☀ THE STORY OF ☀
MARIE CURIE

A Biography Book for New Readers

Written by
Susan B. Katz

Illustrated by
Lindsay Dale Scott

ROCKRIDGE
PRESS

To my dad, Ray—the smartest, kindest, and most humble man I know

Series Designer: Angela Navarra

Interior and Cover Designer: Angela Navarra

Art Producer: Tom Hood

Editor: Eliza Kirby

Production Editor: Mia Moran

Illustrations © 2020 Lindsay Dale Scott

Photography Archive Pics/Alamy, p. 50; History and Art/Alamy, p. 52; Ewing Galloway/Alamy, p. 53 Author photo courtesy of Jeanne Marquis

ISBN: Print 978-1-64739-112-6 | eBook 978-1-64739-113-3

R0

CONTENTS

CHAPTER 1

A NOBEL PRIZE WINNER IS BORN

·✳· Meet Marie Curie ·✳·

Marie Curie was practically born a scientist. Even as a child growing up in Poland, she liked to study science. Sometimes, she put her thumbs in her ears so she would not hear the noise from her sisters and brother. It was easier to read that way. Once, as a joke, her sisters stacked a pile of chairs above and around the table where she sat. Marie didn't notice, because she was so focused on the book she was reading.

When Marie stood up, the chairs crashed down! Marie just shook her head at her sisters and said they were silly for playing a trick on her.

All that studying paid off when she grew up. Determined and smart, Marie did science experiments to learn more about chemical **elements**. She discovered some elements that no other scientist had ever found before. One was **radium**, used in x-rays and to help treat some patients who have **cancer**. Marie spent many hours in the laboratory doing experiments on radium. She discovered another unknown element, **polonium**, too. Even though Marie was one of only a few female scientists in her day, she did not let that stop her. She started out as one of four daughters in a poor, Polish family, and ended up becoming the first woman ever to earn not one, but two **Nobel Prize** awards for her discoveries in two different fields of science: **physics** and **chemistry**.

✳ Marie's Poland ✳

Marie was born Marya Salomee Skłodowska on November 7, 1867, in Warsaw, Poland. She was the youngest of five children. Marie's family and her teachers called her by the nickname Manya. She was very proud to be Polish. By 1877, the **Russian Empire** had taken over parts of Poland.

Many Polish people, including Marie and her family, wished they were free again in their own country. Her father was punished by the Russians for not supporting them enough. He secretly taught in the Polish language, instead of in Russian, so he lost his job as a principal. Marie and her family had to move from their big house into a small, cramped apartment. Her mother, Bronisława, and father, Władysław, raised Marie, her three sisters, and one brother in that tiny

> " I am among those who think that science has **great beauty.** "

4

apartment, which they also used as a **boarding school** to earn money. Up to 10 boys at a time would live with them while Mr. Skłodowski taught them.

Marie fought against the Russian **oppression** of Polish people. There are now stamps and coins with her picture on them and streets named after her. In fact, Marie paved the way for women scientists all over the world and became the most famous female **physicist** of all time!

WHEN?

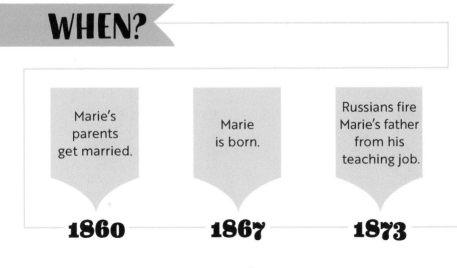

Marie's parents get married.

Marie is born.

Russians fire Marie's father from his teaching job.

1860 — **1867** — **1873**

CHAPTER 2

THE EARLY YEARS

❋ Growing Up in Warsaw ❋

As a child, Marie stood in front of her father's locked, glass cabinet, fascinated by all the beakers, tubes, and other physics equipment. At the age of four, Marie showed how smart she was by teaching herself how to read. Her siblings were shocked, and Marie started crying because of how they reacted. She thought she was doing something wrong! Soon, Marie began helping her older brother and sisters with their math homework. Education was very important to her parents. Mr. and Mrs. Skłodowski also wanted their kids to learn Polish in order to keep their culture and language alive.

Sadly, Marie's mom got sick. She had **tuberculosis**, a disease that makes it hard to breathe and is very **contagious**. Marie's mother made the tough decision to not hug or kiss her children so they wouldn't catch the illness. That made Marie miss her mother even though she was still there. She longed for a hug or to sit in her mother's lap.

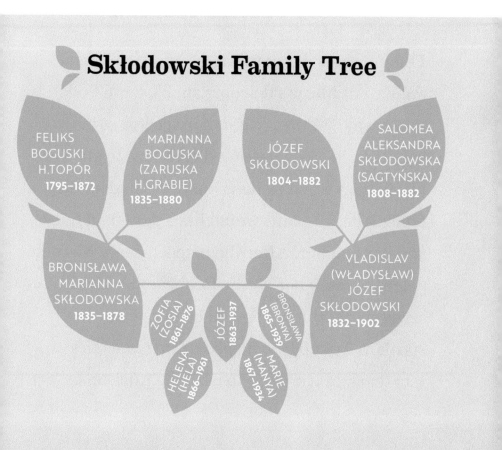

Skłodowski Family Tree

FELIKS BOGUSKI H.TOPÓR
1795–1872

MARIANNA BOGUSKA (ZARUSKA H.GRABIE)
1835–1880

JÓZEF SKŁODOWSKI
1804–1882

SALOMEA ALEKSANDRA SKŁODOWSKA (SAGTYŃSKA)
1808–1882

BRONISŁAWA MARIANNA SKŁODOWSKA
1835–1878

ZOFIA (ZOSIA)
1861–1876

JÓZEF
1863–1937

BRONISŁAWA (BRONYA)
1865–1939

VLADISLAV (WŁADYSŁAW) JÓZEF SKŁODOWSKI
1832–1902

HELENA (HELA)
1866–1961

MARIE (MANYA)
1867–1934

> Nothing in life is to be feared. **It is only to be understood.** Now is the time to understand more, so that we may fear less.

✳ Gold Medal Winner ✳

The Russians did not want children to learn Polish, but Marie's teachers snuck some Polish in anyway. When a Russian **inspector** came to her class, the teacher called on Marie to answer. Marie responded in Russian. If she had spoken Polish, the Russians would have punished her and her teacher. After the inspector left, Marie's teacher kissed her on the forehead. She had saved them! But Marie had been so afraid to speak in front of the inspector that she burst into tears. Marie grew to hate the Russians.

When she was older, Marie and her best friend, Kazia, would walk by a Russian statue in the town square and spit on it!

Her father kept tutoring boys in their home. The boarding students brought in money, but they also brought in a sickness called **typhus**. When Marie was just eight years old, her sister Zosia got sick from the disease and died. This made Marie very sad. Then, just when Marie thought things couldn't get any worse, two years later, her mother also passed away. Marie wore Zosia's coat to her mother's funeral. She fell into a **depression**, which meant she was sad most of the time. Aside from studying, she didn't want to do much else but cry and sleep. Still, Marie's father decided to send her to a private school because she was so smart. Marie graduated first in her class and got a gold medal.

Marie showed the medal to her dad, who was proud. Even though she had **achieved** her goal,

she returned to her bed, still deeply sad about losing her mother and sister. This worried her father.

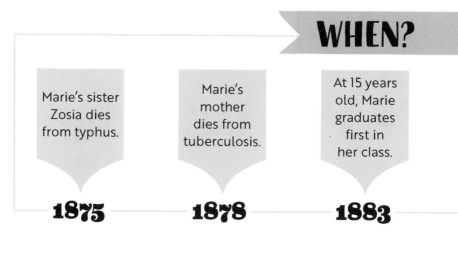

WHEN?

Marie's sister Zosia dies from typhus.

1875

Marie's mother dies from tuberculosis.

1878

At 15 years old, Marie graduates first in her class.

1883

CHAPTER 3

TRAVELING AND LEARNING

Country Living

JUMP
—IN THE—
THINK
TANK

How does being out in nature make you happy? What about nature do you enjoy? Is it the fresh air, animals and birds, or freedom to explore?

Marie's father saw how smart she was, but he also knew she was still very depressed. So, he sent Marie to live with relatives in the Southern Poland countryside, near the Carpathian Mountains. Marie loved being out in nature. The mountains, farms, and castles she explored with her cousins made Marie happier. For the first time, Marie was able to really relax and enjoy life. She rode on a horse-drawn sleigh and danced the **mazurka**—a traditional Polish dance. In fact, one night she danced for so long that she wore out her shoes and had to throw them away! Marie read **fiction** novels. She said that, for a while, she forgot math like **geometry** or **algebra** even existed.

At 16 years old, Marie didn't know what her next step might be, but she returned to Warsaw to keep learning. While her brother went off to **university**, Marie and her sisters couldn't. After Russia took over Poland, women and girls weren't allowed to study at the college level. Marie needed to hatch a plan to keep on studying.

✳ The Flying University ✳

There were signs that said, "No women or girls allowed," at the universities. But Marie wasn't going to give up on her dreams. Marie loved a quote from the author Eliza Orzeszkowa, who said, "a woman possesses the same rights as a man . . . to learning and knowledge." Other people agreed. In 1884, Marie and her sister

Bronya started studying at what was known as the "**Flying University**." It was sometimes also called the Floating University. Female teachers taught classes in their homes. They moved if the Russian government found out where they were.

Marie and Bronya became tutors in Warsaw to earn money and continue studying. Marie also took a job as a **governess**, or nanny, with a rich family. But she did not like how they treated her, so she quit. How would she and Bronya ever earn enough money to attend university? Marie came up with a plan! Bronya would go to Paris, France, to become a doctor, while Marie earned

MYTH & FACT

Marie liked math and science equally.

After Marie left home, her father continued sending her hard math problems. Eventually, she wrote him to say she liked science better.

money and sent it to her. Then they would
switch places so Marie could become a scientist.

Bronya agreed and Marie found a job with a
kinder family. At night, she would study physics
and math. Marie also took on a dangerous project
during that time. She started teaching Polish
children how to read and write in Polish. It was

risky but, like her parents, Marie wanted to keep Polish culture and language alive. At that time, she also got her first chance to work in a lab at a secret museum in Warsaw. That inspired her to keep working hard. She was determined to go to university and become a scientist.

WHEN?

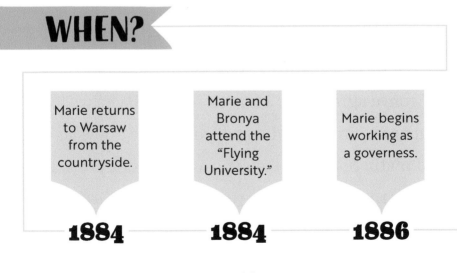

Marie returns to Warsaw from the countryside.

Marie and Bronya attend the "Flying University."

Marie begins working as a governess.

1884 — **1884** — **1886**

CHAPTER 4

PARIS, AT LAST

✳ The Sorbonne ✳

In 1891, Bronya graduated from the Faculty of
Medicine, and was one of only three women out
of 1,000 students! She finally sent for her sister.
Marie was scared, but she was also inspired by
Bronya. She held tight to her dream of becoming
a scientist and set out for Sorbonne University
and a new life in Paris. Marie had saved up
money for almost eight years and now her plan
was working. At just 23 years old, she packed up
her clothes, a feather mattress, some food, water,
and a stool to sit on. After a tiring four-day train
ride, Bronya's husband, Casimir, met Marie at
the train station.

Soon, Bronya took her to sign up for classes.
Marie was still using her Polish nickname,
Manya. Since she was starting over in Paris,
she decided to use the French version, Marie.

After a while, Marie moved into her own apartment, but she didn't have very much money so the apartment had no heat. It was so cold that water froze when it filled her sink!

The next year, Marie got a better apartment and a job at the Society for the Encouragement of National Industry. While she was studying, Marie also started her research on the chemistry of steel.

At that time, there were not many women studying, and Marie faced a lot of **sexism**, or unfair treatment based on a person's gender. Some people didn't believe women could become scientists, but Marie wouldn't let that stop her. Others, like her professor Gabriel Lippmann, believed in Marie. He helped her get **grant** money to keep studying steel. Marie graduated second in her whole class with a degree in mathematics. She was one of only two women who graduated at all. She also got a **scholarship** to study for another year.

> We must have **perseverance** and above all confidence in ourselves. We must believe that we are gifted for something and that this thing must be attained.

✳ Love and Magnetism ✳

Marie spent the next year at the Sorbonne studying math and science. She was one of 23 women in the School of Sciences which had over 2,000 students. Marie studied **magnetism**, or how two metals are pulled together or pushed apart. Although she worked alone, Marie was happy. She was living her dream as an independent woman and serious scientist. The only problem was that there wasn't enough space in Professor Lippmann's lab for her equipment. Luckily, a

JUMP
—IN THE—
THINK
TANK

Do you have a sister, brother, cousin, or friend who inspires you? How do they make a path for you to follow?

friend of Bronya's suggested Marie meet a physicist named Pierre Curie. He had invented some tools that might help Marie with her research.

Pierre did not have a lab, but he did offer to give Marie advice and let her use the state-of-the-art **electrometer** he had invented with his brother, Paul-Jacques. Shortly after they met, Marie and Pierre realized how much they had in common. They fell in love and got married on July 26, 1895. Pierre described her as "a woman of genius" who understood his "nature and soul." The two newlyweds rode off from their wedding on bicycles and traveled around Brittany and France for their honeymoon.

Marie had promised her father she'd return to Poland but, instead, she and Pierre decided to

start their new life together in Paris. Both Pierre and Marie liked to work in their labs without being around very many people.

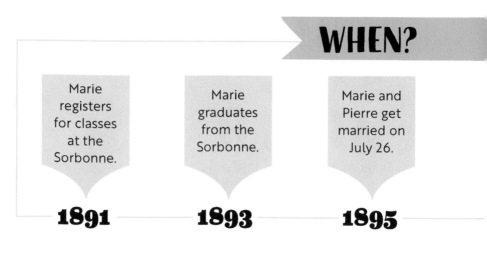

WHEN?

Marie registers for classes at the Sorbonne.	Marie graduates from the Sorbonne.	Marie and Pierre get married on July 26.
1891	**1893**	**1895**

CHAPTER 5

A WORLD OF ELEMENTS

❋ Radioactive ❋

Marie wanted to continue studying and earn
the highest degree, a **doctorate**. To do this, she
needed to make an important **discovery**. Pierre
helped Marie get a lab near his office. As a new
wife in the 1800s, Marie was also expected to
cook and clean. While working on her research,
Marie had a baby girl named Irène. Now Marie
was a mother, wife, and scientist.

Many scientists, including Marie, studied the
elements. Everything in nature is made up of a
single element or of different elements joined
together. Marie knew a lot about the **periodic
table**, a chart of elements created by the famous
chemist Dmitri Mendeleev. For over 25 years,
scientists had believed that only 63 elements
made up everything in nature. Several new ones
were added, thanks to Marie and other scientists.
Today, there are 118 elements on the chart.

One physicist, Antoine Henri Becquerel, discovered that the element **uranium** gives off invisible rays. This interested Marie. She decided to do more research. She did experiments and noticed invisible rays coming from some natural material. She measured the rays and named them **"radioactivity."**

Scientists at the famous Academy of Sciences in Paris wanted to hear about Marie's research, but women were not allowed to present information there. Gabriel Lippmann, her professor and friend, shared her research. Marie's ideas got attention, but scientists wanted proof that radioactivity came from individual elements. Marie got to work. She needed to **isolate**, or separate, the radioactive elements to prove they existed.

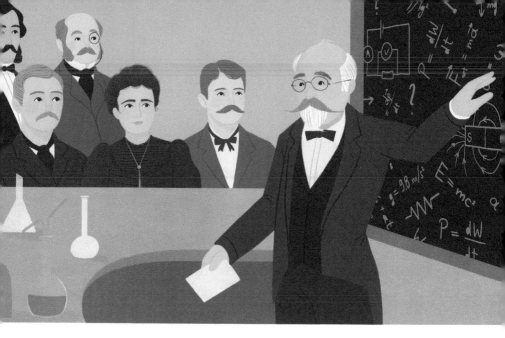

✳ **The Discovery** ✳

Marie's research required a lot of concentration and patience. She sat for hours testing how much radiation an element gave off. Marie's husband, Pierre, was so interested that he started to work with her. Marie used Pierre's electrometer and **chronometer** to measure radioactive rays from different natural materials. Marie recorded information, including how strong the rays were. She also recorded how a ray's energy changed at different temperatures, and in different forms, like when it was a liquid or a solid.

Marie tested **pitchblende**, a heavy, black material used to make pottery and glass. She knew that pitchblende was a combination of oxygen and uranium. Marie also knew oxygen did not give off radioactive rays, while uranium did. She discovered the radioactive rays coming from the pitchblende were stronger than pure uranium. This meant that there was another element in pitchblende, and it was even more radioactive than uranium.

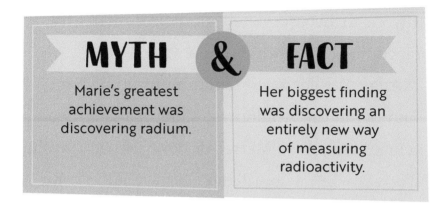

MYTH & FACT

MYTH: Marie's greatest achievement was discovering radium.

FACT: Her biggest finding was discovering an entirely new way of measuring radioactivity.

By March of 1898, Marie had proven that several minerals gave off more rays than pure uranium. So, in April of 1898, she wrote another paper. Her discovery changed the way radioactivity was measured. Some of the materials Marie wrote about were as much as 400 times more radioactive than uranium. She also discovered two new elements. In July of 1898, the Curies discovered polonium. They named it after Marie's homeland of Poland. Then, in December, they discovered radium. Radium was a key find for Marie since it was 900 times more radioactive than uranium. It was a huge deal for anyone to discover a new element and an even bigger deal for a woman scientist!

Again, Professor Lippmann presented her findings at the Academy of Sciences. But many scientists doubted Marie's discoveries because she was a woman who still did not have a doctorate degree. Pierre thought that even Becquerel looked down on her simply because she was a woman! But, despite others' doubts, Marie's discoveries would change her life and the world. She was about to become one of the most important scientists in history.

WHEN?

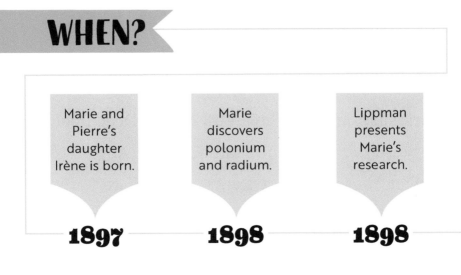

Marie and Pierre's daughter Irène is born.

1897

Marie discovers polonium and radium.

1898

Lippman presents Marie's research.

1898

CHAPTER 6

THE FAMOUS CURIES

·✳· **Pure Radium** ·✳·

Once Marie had discovered radium, she needed to isolate it, or pull it apart. Starting in 1899, she spent countless hours in the lab racing to prove that radium was real and more radioactive than any other element. She wanted to get to her goal before any other scientists did. Marie worked tirelessly and Pierre began to worry about her health. Not only was she researching around the clock but, sometimes she was so focused, she did not eat or sleep. The Curies did not know it at the time, but Marie was literally risking her life every day to advance science. The radioactive materials she was touching, weighing, and moving around were very dangerous.

Pierre begged fellow scientists for money and a laboratory. They were given a hangar that had been first used to park airplanes, which was a larger space than they had before. They also hired an assistant named André-Louis Debierne. Marie was so determined to isolate radium that she felt like it became a dream. By 1902, Marie and Pierre had isolated enough radium to prove its existence. On June 25, 1903, she earned her doctorate from the Sorbonne. She was the first woman in France to achieve this advanced degree—she was now Dr. Marie Curie!

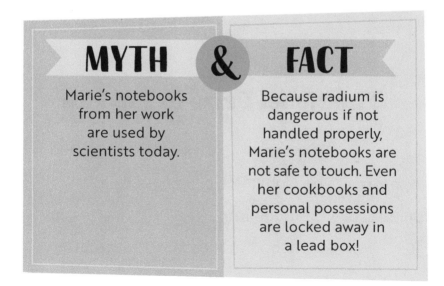

MYTH & FACT

Marie's notebooks from her work are used by scientists today.

Because radium is dangerous if not handled properly, Marie's notebooks are not safe to touch. Even her cookbooks and personal possessions are locked away in a lead box!

⁂ The Nobel Prize in Physics ⁂

Back then, there were few awards for great
scientists. The Nobel Prize, recognizing
scientists who made important discoveries, had
just been established in 1901. Two years later,
in 1903, Antoine Henri Becquerel and Pierre
Curie were sent a letter giving them the Nobel

Prize for finding polonium and radium. It did not mention Marie, even though three of the four men who wrote the letter knew she had done the research. Marie was especially shocked that one of the men was Professor Lippmann, her trusted advisor and friend! Some people thought that Becquerel had encouraged the committee members to leave Marie out so he could get more credit.

Pierre wrote back saying he would not accept the prize unless Marie was included. The committee changed their minds and, in November of 1903, the Curies finally received an invitation for both of them to come get the Nobel Prize in Sweden. They accepted the prize but decided not to make the trip. Marie's father had passed away, and she was

depressed and too sad to travel so far. Becquerel got the award at a ceremony and was given all the credit that night, even though Pierre and Marie did all the work. Even so, Marie became the first woman to receive a Nobel Prize. She was the only woman to win until her daughter Irène won in 1935.

Marie and Pierre became famous almost overnight. Reporters and photographers came to their lab and followed them everywhere.

They did not like the distraction from their research. Marie and Pierre also began having health problems because of how much they worked with radium. Luckily, Marie was still healthy enough to give birth to their second daughter, Ève, in 1904.

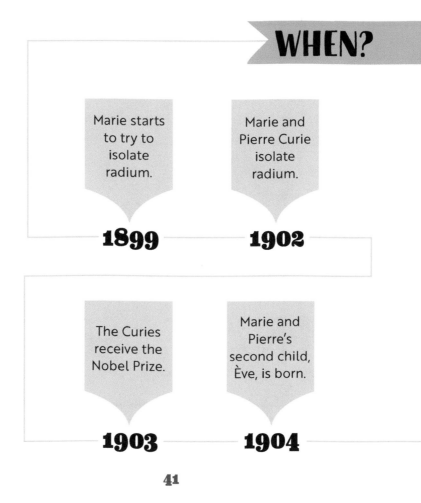

WHEN?

Marie starts to try to isolate radium.

1899

Marie and Pierre Curie isolate radium.

1902

The Curies receive the Nobel Prize.

1903

Marie and Pierre's second child, Ève, is born.

1904

CHAPTER 7

A GENIUS AT WORK

Pain in the Public Eye

In 1905, Marie and Pierre traveled to Sweden. Pierre gave a Nobel Prize lecture, explaining the research they had done together and the research Marie had done alone. Then they returned to their busy life in Paris. Sadly, on April 19, 1906, Pierre was killed by a horse-drawn carriage in Paris. Marie was devastated, but she took over Pierre's teaching job at the Sorbonne, becoming the first female professor there. This was such a big deal that, on November 5, 1906, people lined up to see Madame Curie teach. Marie and her family moved outside of Paris. She had to take a train to the lab every day, but Marie couldn't bear to live in the house without Pierre.

Meanwhile, scientists were making important discoveries in **atomic physics**. Marie became interested in that field as well. She no longer had Pierre as her partner in life or in the lab, but she worked with other scientists, including

Albert Einstein. Andrew Carnegie, a wealthy **philanthropist**, was impressed with Marie and her work. In 1907, he created the Curie Scholarships, which paid for scientists to help her in the lab. In 1911, Marie was nominated to become a member of the Academy of Sciences in France, which was only open to men before then. She ran against two men and lost by one vote! Marie never applied again, and it would be 68 more years before a woman was allowed in.

In 1911, Marie was awarded a second Nobel Prize in chemistry for isolating radium. But the committee wanted Marie to turn down her second

Nobel Prize because people were spreading gossip and rumors about her. Marie wrote to them and said her personal life had nothing to do with her scientific accomplishments. She was the only person—not just the only woman—ever to earn two Nobel Prizes! Soon after, the **Pasteur Institute** built a new lab at the University of Paris especially for Marie. The Radium Institute had two sections: One let Marie continue her research, while the other, Pasteur Laboratory, studied the use of radium in cancer treatment.

JUMP
—IN THE—
THINK TANK

Has anyone ever spread rumors about you? Whether they were true or not, who stood by you? Your family? Friends? How did that feel?

✳ **Marie the Hero** ✳

Marie's health continued to get worse. She became so sick that she went to recover in England. She came back to Paris in 1912. In 1914, World War I began. Marie was worried about bombings and feared losing her supply of radium, so she hid it in a bank safe.

Marie wanted to help during the war. She knew x-raying soldiers' bones on the battlefield would help save lives, but x-rays were only available in hospitals. With the help of the Red Cross, Marie had a truck made into an x-ray machine, which she drove to help injured soldiers. Then, she asked other women to let her convert their cars into 20 mobile x-ray machines known as "little Curies." Marie became a war hero!

In 1920, Marie met an American reporter named Mrs. Meloney who changed her life.

In an interview, Marie told Mrs. Meloney she did not have enough money to buy more radium to continue her research. It cost $100,000 for just a gram. Mrs. Meloney asked American women to donate. In less than a year, they raised more than $150,000.

Radiation treatment was soon curing cancer in patients around the world. But radium hurt

> " You cannot hope to build a better world without improving the individuals. To that end, each of us must work for his own improvement . . . "

Marie's eyesight and hearing and caused her to get anemia, a blood disease. Sadly, Marie died in 1934, but her important work has saved many lives. She lives on as one of the most accomplished scientists of all time.

WHEN?

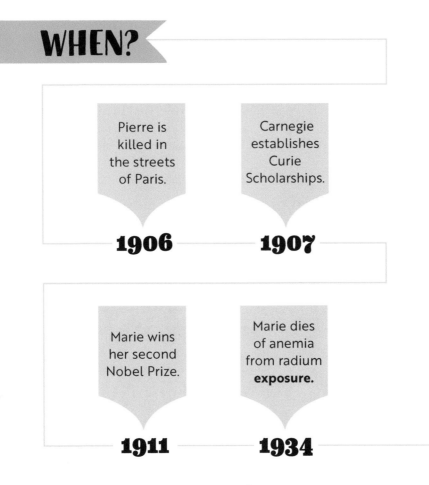

Pierre is killed in the streets of Paris.

1906

Carnegie establishes Curie Scholarships.

1907

Marie wins her second Nobel Prize.

1911

Marie dies of anemia from radium **exposure.**

1934

CHAPTER 8

SO . . . WHO WAS MARIE CURIE?

Challenge Accepted!

Now that you know so much about Marie's life and work, let's test your new knowledge in a little who, what, when, where, why, and how quiz. Feel free to look back in the text to find the answers if you need to, but try to remember first!

1 **Where was Marie born?**

→ A   Warsaw, Poland

→ B   Paris, France

→ C   London, England

→ D   New York, New York

2 **What was the name of the "moving" school in Poland that Marie and her sister attended?**

→ A   The Dancing University

→ B   The Science University

→ C   The Flying University

→ D   The Math University

3 **Where did Bronya and Marie go to school in Paris?**

→ A   University of Paris

→ B   Curie University

→ C   The University of Michigan

→ D   The Sorbonne

4 **Who was Marie's mentor and professor who eventually turned on her?**

→ A   Professor Lippmann

→ B   Professor Einstein

→ C   Professor Nobel

→ D   Professor Curie

5 **What elements did Marie discover?**

→ A   Carbon and nitrogen

→ B   Polonium and radium

→ C   Hydrogen and oxygen

→ D   Magnesium and sodium

6 **What were Marie and Pierre's daughters' names?**

→ A   Bronya and Zosia
→ B   Laverne and Shirley
→ C   Irène and Ève
→ D   Maya and Rosa

7 **Who was the famous scientist Marie collaborated with?**

→ A   Ada Lovelace
→ B   Henry Ford
→ C   Jane Goodall
→ D   Albert Einstein

8 **What major discovery did Marie make that changed the scientific community?**

→ A   Radioactivity
→ B   Gravitational pull
→ C   Electricity
→ D   Microscopes

9 **How did Marie help soldiers and doctors during World War I?**

→ A She took radium to them.

→ B She made mobile x-ray cars for use on the battlefield.

→ C She invented a vaccine.

→ D She cured cancer.

10 **Which prize was Marie the only person to ever win twice?**

→ A An Academy Award

→ B An Oscar

→ C An Emmy

→ D The Nobel Prize

※ **Our World** ※

Marie's scientific discoveries influenced our world today. Let's look at a few things that are different because of Marie's work.

→ X-ray machines are now smaller and can be used outside of hospitals, such as at football games and small clinics. Marie helped make x-rays available to patients. It is important that doctors can see a broken bone in order to set it in a cast or do surgery to fix it.

→ Radium and radioactive material are needed for radiation treatment for cancer patients. Millions of sick people benefit from Marie's research when they get radiation treatment for all different types of cancer. Marie was the first to discover that radium and radioactivity existed. Without her talent, we may never have found a way to treat cancer.

→ Scholarships and labs all over the world have been created to continue Marie's groundbreaking research. She also inspired, and still inspires, women and girls to study science and math. Marie didn't let anyone else's limitations stop her from fulfilling her dream. Why should you?

JUMP
—IN THE—
THINK
TANK
FOR

MORE!

Now let's think a little more about what Marie did and how her work and determination have affected the world we currently live in.

→ How did Marie's research, and the attention she got for it, help other scientists work toward a cure for cancer?

→ How does Marie's determination inspire you to ignore people who say women shouldn't study science?

→ How did Marie overcome her sadness and depression to do her best in the lab? How can you push past that feeling to keep at a goal?

Glossary

achieved: Accomplished something you set out to do

algebra: The part of mathematics in which letters and other symbols are used to represent numbers in equations

atomic physics: The field of physics that studies atoms as an isolated system of electrons and an atomic nucleus

boarding school: A place where students live and study, staying away from home

cancer: A group of diseases involving abnormal cell growth that can spread to other parts of the body and do harm

chemistry: The study of the properties of matter, how and why substances mix or separate to form other substances, and how they interact with energy

chronometer: An instrument for measuring time, especially one meant to keep accurate time regardless of motion or variations in temperature, humidity, and air pressure

contagious: Spreading a disease from one person to another

depression: A serious, but treatable, mental illness that makes you feel sad and lose interest in activities you once enjoyed

discovery: Something that nobody knew before

doctorate: The highest degree you can earn in graduate school. One type of a doctorate is a PhD, which Marie earned.

electrometer: An instrument for measuring electric charge or electrical potential difference

element: A substance, or atom, with the same number of protons in their atomic nuclei. In total, 118 elements have been identified.

exposure: The act of coming into contact with something

fiction: Literature, including short stories and novels, describing imaginary events and people

Flying University: An underground school system that functioned from 1885 to 1905 in Warsaw, Poland

geometry: The study in math of shapes, angles, planes, lines, and relations of points and lines

governess: A woman employed to teach and take care of children in someone's home

grant: Money given by the government or an organization that is not paid back

inspector: An official employed to ensure that rules are obeyed

isolate: To separate things

magnetism: A force that can pull two metals closer or push them apart

mazurka: A lively, fast Polish dance

Nobel Prize: An international award for scientific discoveries, named after the Swedish scientist, Alfred Nobel

oppression: Cruel or unfair treatment

Pasteur Institute: A French foundation dedicated to the study of biology, micro-organisms, diseases, and vaccines, named after the scientist Louis Pasteur

periodic table: A chart organizing and naming all of the chemical elements, arranged by atomic number

philanthropist: A person who gives money and time to help others, especially by donating money to good causes

physicist: An expert in or person who studies physics

physics: A branch of science dealing with how matter is structured and how the elements of the universe interact

pitchblende: A form of the mineral uraninite found in brown or black masses that contains radium

polonium: A rare and highly radioactive metal discovered by Marie and Pierre Curie

radioactivity: The release of ionizing radiation or particles

radium: A naturally occurring radioactive metal formed by the breakdown of uranium and thorium, discovered by Marie and Pierre Curie

Russian Empire: A world power that controlled many areas in Europe, Asia, and North America

scholarship: Money given to support a student's studies

sexism: Laws or rules that are prejudiced, or discriminate, usually against women, because of gender

tuberculosis (TB): A disease caused by bacteria that usually attacks the lungs and can also damage other parts of the body. TB spreads when a person with TB coughs, sneezes, or talks.

typhus: A group of infectious diseases that cause symptoms including fever, headache, and a rash

university: A college, school, or institution of higher education and research that awards academic degrees

uranium: A radioactive metal, used today as a fuel in nuclear reactors

Bibliography

American Institute of Physics. "Marie Curie and the Science of Radioactivity." Accessed February 19, 2020. History.AIP.org/exhibits/curie/stud1.htm.

Encyclopedia Britannica (online). "Marie Curie." Last modified March 4, 2020. Britannica.com/biography/Marie-Curie.

Eschner, Kat. "Three Quirky Facts About Marie Curie." *Smithsonian Magazine* (online). November 7, 2017. SmithsonianMag.com/smart-news /three-quirky-facts-about-marie-curie-180967075.

Funk, Tyler. "The Life of Madame Marie Curie—A Brief Biographical History of One of the World's Greatest Scientific Minds." Owlcation. Last modified November 6, 2013. Owlcation.com/humanities/Madame-Marie-Curie.

Goldsmith, Barbara. *Obsessive Genius: The Inner World of Marie Curie.* New York: Atlas Books, W. W. Norton & Co., 2005.

Killough McClafferty, Carla. *Something Out of Nothing: Marie Curie and Radium.* New York: Farrar, Straus and Giroux, 2006.

Krull, Kathleen. *Giants of Science: Marie Curie.* New York: Viking, 2007.

McHugh, Brendan. "Marie Curie: 7 Facts About the Groundbreaking Scientist." Biography.com. Last modified November 6, 2019. Biography.com /news/marie-curie-biography-facts.

NobelPrize.org. "Marie Curie Documentary." Accessed February 19, 2020. NobelPrize.org/prizes/chemistry/1911/marie-curie/documentary.

Pflaum, Rosalynd. *Grand Obsession: Madame Curie and Her World.* New York: Doubleday, 1989.

Schmidt, Fabian. "The Two-Time Nobel Prize Winner, Marie Curie, was Born 150 Years Ago Today." Deutsche Welle. November 7, 2017. DW.com/en /the-two-time-nobel-prize-winner-marie-curie-was-born-150-years-ago /g-41262435.

Acknowledgments

First and foremost, I want to thank Marie Curie for being such a smart and steadfast scientist, who advanced x-rays and radiation treatments for cancer patients. I appreciate my outstanding editor, Eliza, who entrusted me with this book and guided me with grace, precision, and determination. I appreciate my parents, Janice and Ray, for their encouragement. To my brother, Steve, thanks! Kudos to my talented writers' group—Andrew, Brandi, Evan, Kyle, and Sonia. In memory of my Grandma Grace, my Aunt Judy, Joe McClain, and my mentor, Ilse. To my nephews Sam, Jacob, and David and my nieces, Sofia & Katherine. Thanks to the entire Callisto team! I am supported by family and friends: Michelle G., Susan, Ann & Greg, Danielle, Jeanne, Deborah, Kiernan, Laurie, Tanya, Carla, Julia & Ira, Maureen, Amparo, Michael, Ricardo, Alejandra, Arden, Jen, Tami, Karen, Annie, Crystal, Bryan, Jessica, Marji, Marcy, Lara, Anita & Bob, Jerry, Nena & Mel, Jami, Stacy & Rick, Laura & Darren, Michelle R., Chalmers, Violeta, Diana y Juanca, and Sylvia Boorstein.

—SBK

About the Author

SUSAN B. KATZ is an award-winning bilingual author, National Board Certified Teacher, educational consultant, and keynote speaker. She taught for over 25 years. Susan has five published books with Scholastic, Random House, and Barefoot Books. *Meditation Station*, a book about trains and mindfulness, is due out in Fall 2020 with Bala Books (Shambhala). Her other titles include: *ABC, Baby Me!*, *My Mama Earth* (Moonbeam Gold Award Winner for Best Picture Book and named "Top Green Toy" by Education. com), *ABC School's for Me* (illustrated by Lynn Munsinger), and *All Year Round*, which she translated into Spanish as *Un Año Redondo* for Scholastic. She also authored *The Story of Ruth Bader Ginsburg*, *The Story of Frida Kahlo*, *The Story of Jane Goodall*, and *The Story of Albert Einstein* for Callisto Media. Susan is also the executive director of ConnectingAuthors.org, a national nonprofit bringing children's book authors and illustrators into schools. Ms. Katz served as the strategic partner manager for authors at Facebook. When she's not writing, Susan enjoys traveling, salsa dancing, and spending time at the beach. You can find out more about her books and school visits at **SusanKatzBooks.com**.

About the Illustrator

LINDSAY DALE SCOTT is an illustrator and designer in northeast Ohio. She has done artwork for several children's books, including *Leaves: An Autumn Pop-Up Book* and *Little Vampire's Big Smile* along with tons of greeting cards for American Greetings. She loves drawing animals, birds, and florals, along with historical and decorative figures. She currently lives with her pastor husband Andrew, their two dogs Toby and Violet, two bunnies Sam and Pepper, and their newest addition: their daughter Nora James.

WHO WILL INSPIRE YOU NEXT?

EXPLORE A WORLD OF HEROES AND ROLE MODELS IN
THE STORY OF... BIOGRAPHY SERIES FOR NEW READERS.

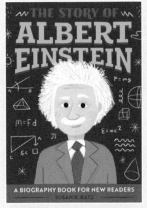

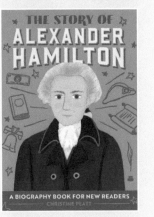

→ LOOK FOR THIS SERIES ←
WHEREVER BOOKS AND EBOOKS ARE SOLD

George Washington	Harriet Tubman
Abraham Lincoln	Barack Obama
Ruth Bader Ginsburg	Helen Keller
Frida Kahlo	Marie Curie